# THE LITTLE BLUE BOOK OF PRAYER

Lionel Blue and Jonathan Magonet first met forty years ago when the former was studying to be a Rabbi and the latter to be a doctor. Both eventually became Rabbis.

Rabbi Dr Jonathan Magonet is the Principal of Leo Baeck college, a Bible scholar and author (as well as being a doctor in medicine and theology). Rabbi Lionel Blue is a broadcaster, author and lecturer at the same seminary, whose morning radio talks have become nationally known and loved.

Together they have also published *A Guide to the Here and Hereafter* and for twenty-five years have prepared the new Liturgy for the Reform Jewish Community. Both are involved in the work of dialogue with their fellow Christians and Muslims. In their spare time Rabbi Dr Magonet composes songs and Rabbi Blue tells jokes.

*Books available from HarperCollins*

*by Lionel Blue*

A Backdoor to Heaven (Fount Paperbacks)

*by Lionel Blue and Jonathan Magonet*

The Guide to the Here and Hereafter
(Fount Paperbacks)

How to Get Up When Life Gets You Down

# *The Little Blue Book of Prayer*

Lionel Blue and Jonathan Magonet

Fount
*An Imprint of* HarperCollins*Publishers*

Fount Paperbacks is an imprint of
HarperCollins*Religious*
Part of HarperCollins*Publishers*
77–85 Fulham Palace Road,
Hammersmith, London W6 8JB

First published in Great Britain
in 1993 by Fount Paperbacks

1 3 5 7 9 10 8 6 4 2



A catalogue record for this book is
available from the British Library

ISBN 0 00 627666 0

Printed and bound in Great Britain by
HarperCollinsManufacturing Glasgow

*For Leslie Shepard*

who helped us keep the metaphysics straight

# CONTENTS

# INTRODUCTION

Prayer – Jewish style – has some special characteristics. For one thing "pray" in Hebrew does not have the same meaning as its equivalent in many European languages, such as English.

"Pray" in Hebrew does not mean "request" or "ask for" but is reflexive. It means something the one who prays does to her- or himself. It is also connected with the word for "judge". It is a work accomplished on oneself, even a self-judgement. Another Hebrew word for prayer also means "work" in the sense of "service", like the use of "service" in English for public prayers.

We work for the good of all God's creatures and society, that is the outer work. But we ourselves are also God's creatures and part of society and so we must work on ourselves too. That is the inner work of self-purification and prayer.

Jewish prayers, therefore, don't ask for much and usually only for general things, but they demand a lot. They can therefore seem austere to religious romantics.

Since the aim of a public Jewish service is to centre our minds on God and others, not on ourselves, after the beginning of the public prayers, the use of the word "I" is not encouraged – it is in fact only used for private prayers and preparatory meditations and in quotations.

Another characteristic of Jewish prayer which can seem strange is the lack of division between prayer and study – also the use of argument and humour when talking to God.

An example of the former is the Shema – the central "prayer" of Judaism. "Hear (*Shema*) Israel, the Lord is our God, the Lord is One." The *rabbis* said if you only have time to pray the words or study them, then you should study them. God knows He is One, and doesn't need to be reminded of it. It is the person who says the prayer who has to absorb it.

Examples of holy argument and humour are scattered throughout the Bible and later Jewish literature down to modern times. Answering back is not a mark of disrespect or disbelief but of trust. Your own truth is holy, like any other truth, for God is truth.

Now this little book is meant for everybody and for mainly private use. You don't have to be Jewish to use it or get some benefit from it, though the prayers in the book were written by Jews, defined widely and generously, and many of them are from the Jewish liturgy. Because of this, we have emphasized general and personal prayers, omitting technical, liturgical or theological terms, and adapting them to the needs of anyone living somewhere, somehow. To help with the "translation" we have provided a glossary at the back which explains a few terms and tells a little bit more about the people quoted.

These prayers are not meant to be recited word by word. Praying other people's prayers is like wearing their clothes – a lot of attention and adjustment is required. Regard them as suggestions, as start-offs, if you find prayer embarrassing or awkward. Relax, give yourself time, and let whatever speaks inside you have its say. Don't worry if the inner voice is muffled by a lot of fluff, some of it rather unpleasant.

Prayers are also affected by the sexual revolution. When most of the quoted prayers were written, God was definitely a "He". Actually "He" was always a "She" and an "It" too, but this knowledge was kept to theologians. Now it is general. So whenever "He" is mentioned, make your own appropriate adjustments.

As well as a "He" ("She" or "It"), there is also an "I" who has written the commentary. This "I" is a composite character who speaks for both the editors – Rabbi Lionel Blue and Rabbi Jonathan Magonet. To their surprise, for both have very different temperaments, "I" is reasonably consistent, and does not seem to suffer from split personality.

One reason, maybe, is that they have worked together as editors of *Forms of Prayer* – the liturgy of the Reform Synagogues of Great Britain – for nearly twenty-five years. Many of their translations and compositions are taken from that work which has been a source of excitement, exasperation, exaltation, worry, contentment, and gratitude for a huge part of their working lives. It is good to pass on the pleasure and piety to a wider community.

They would therefore like to express their gratitude with this slim volume to the Reform Synagogues of Great Britain which made it possible. Thanks also to Jean Myers, Rose and Peter Towell.

# *Thoughts on Prayer*

## *What Is Prayer?*

There is often a tension between the "official" collective prayers of a religious community and the private prayer that we bring to God ourselves. When the Temple in Jerusalem was destroyed, the sacrifices were replaced by formal services and rituals – prayer became "the service of the heart". But that still left room for meeting God privately, "outside office hours".

**So what is prayer?**
It doesn't have to be services or words, though it can be both.

It can be a feeling that God is present.
It doesn't have to include asking for anything.
It can be just awe or wonder, or a wave of affection breaking over you.
It can be like plugging into an electric current.
It can change while you are praying.
It can be surprise.
It can be . . . Fill in the rest from your own experience.

Here's what other Jewish teachers say:

> Prayer is our humble answer to the inconceivable surprise of living.
>
> Abraham Joshua Heschel

Words are just the outer shell, meditation is the inner kernel. The words we pray are the body, but meditation is the soul.

Bachya

We do not even know how we are supposed to pray. All we do is call for help because of the need of the moment. But what the soul intends is spiritual need, only we are not able to express what the soul means. That is why we do not merely ask God to hear our call for help, but also beg Him who knows what is hidden, to hear the silent cry of the soul.

Martin Buber

## *How To Pray*

You don't have to grovel.

You don't need a beginning or ending. Amens optional!

You don't have to have a book.

A glass of wine or a little bit of brandy can help to hot it up (if you're not an alcoholic).

You don't have to stand up, sit down, stand up, sit down, stand up and other ritual bobbings.

You can enjoy it like love play or peanut butter or truffles.

You can say it with song or silence.

You can ask God to sit at the bottom of your bed (as it were).

You can think of God as your baby, lover, mistress, mother, father, your friend and even your foe. They all have their uses. They are all "as if".

You can pray in a bar, a bath, a bus stop, or a kitchen.

You can remember God (which is prayer) by clasping something. Patients in pain in hospital often haven't got words, but they get comfort from clasping their prayer-book, Bible or religious object, and that "clasping" is also prayer.

## *Silence*

**Layers of silence**

Prayer is a two-way activity. If God exists you don't have to do it all. You're not a human prayerwheel over-fulfilling your norm, or a spiritual athlete running another lap around the liturgy.

"Be still and know that I am God." (Psalm 46:10)

So be silent, and let God do the work.

Lots of people find silence is complex and comes in layers. This is my own experience of it:

First, self-consciousness, screwing up eyes and embarrassment, then –

Trivia and anxieties: Have I left the light on? Did I pay the telephone bill? then –

Embarrassment: Remembering failures, economic, sexual and personal, then –

Anger and nastiness, difficult to admit what I am, then –

Self-pity – sometimes tears, then –

Exhaustion and emptiness . . . then –

A bird sings, or a carhorn honks in the distance, then –

Catharsis. Peacefulness. You open your eyes. Everything seems just right as it is. Occasionally you plug into joy.

You can say this Psalm as an introduction or finale to your silence.

O Lord, my heart is not proud,
my eyes are not ambitious.
I am not busy with things too great
or too wonderful for me.

Have I not set my soul
in quietness and peace;
like a child at its mother's breast,
my soul is like a weaned child.

O Israel, hope in the Lord
now and for ever!

Psalm 131

Don't fret if your heart is rather proud, and your eyes are a bit ambitious. They'll get sorted out in the silence. If they don't, then don't suppress them, but give them your attention. That's what God may want of you.

## *Preparing To Pray*

When does prayer begin? Some people try to prepare for public prayer with private prayer and meditation. It doesn't work for me! What works is the opposite. After the public service ends, for the first time I can pray – really pray. The service is the preparation to prayer, not vice versa.

You have to find out what turns you on. Some mystics used to sing and sway (a little self-hypnosis helps concentration).

Here are some of my own turn-ons and turn-offs.

*Turn-ons*
Need
After a row
After making love
Fright
When the stock market plunges
Cemeteries
Washing up after a party

*Turn-offs*
Taped religious music
Random dippings into the Bible
Being watched while I pray
Religious people around me
Formal services – weddings, school prayers, commemoration services etc. – when there is too much expectation around.

## *Lessons About Prayer From The Holocaust*

*May God remember our martyrs . . .*
We remember our six million dead and all who died when evil ruled the world. We remember those we knew and those whose very name is lost.

We mourn for all that died with them; their goodness and their wisdom, which could have saved the world and healed so many wounds. We mourn for the genius and the wit that died, the learning and the laughter that were lost. The world has become a poorer place, and our hearts grow cold as we think of the splendour that might have been.

We stand in gratitude for their example of decency and goodness. They are like candles which shine out from the darkness of those years, and in their light we know what goodness is – and evil.

We salute those men and women who were not Jews, who had the courage to stand outside the mob and suffer with us. They, too, are Your witnesses, a source of hope when we despair.

In silence we remember those who sanctified God's name on earth in dark times.

There must have been hundreds and thousands of prayers or millions, said by people on their way to the concentration camps or queuing in front of gas chambers, and they weren't answered in any way we can understand. Where was God? We don't know.

But a few prayers provide the beginnings of an answer by their very existence.

Here are some:

O Lord, remember not only the men and women of goodwill but also those of illwill. But do not remember the suffering they have inflicted upon us; remember the fruits we brought thanks to this suffering, our comradeship, our loyalty, our humility, the courage, the generosity, the greatness of hearts which have grown out of this; and when they come to judgment, let all the fruits that we have borne be their forgiveness.

The prayer of an unknown woman, found on a piece of wrapping paper in Ravensbruck concentration camp

I believe in the sun even when it is not shining.
I believe in love even when feeling it not.
I believe in God even when He is silent.

Inscription on the walls of a cellar in Cologne, Germany, where Jews hid from the Nazis

## *Prayers Without Words*

Some mystics held that the words of a prayer were only its outer shell. As they were repeated they turned into song and as the song was repeated, all words died anyway and only the tune was left. And even that became voiceless as it transferred from the mouth and throat to the heart. The prayer had become a silent song, hummed within. Sometimes it turned into an ecstatic dance.

In our society ecstatic dances seem contrived or pop, but inner hums are convenient prayers while waiting for a bus or on a late-night station platform.

Any tune will do if you direct it to heaven.

## *Prayer Boomerangs*

Prayers can act like boomerangs. We get incensed by this or that, and indignantly ask God to do something about it, to take a hand in it as it were. But God is spirit and has no hands in the human sense. But if He has no hands, how can He intervene? And then the realization comes, we are His hands. Our prayer boomerangs back on us.

Or we ask God, because we're honest, to help us win the lottery or the football pools. And while we pray, we can't help thinking of the refugees and starving to whom our relative poverty is wealth beyond imagining. What should we do about it? It's an uncomfortable thought, but in a backhanded way our selfish prayer has been answered. God has fielded it back to us, turned it inside out.

Lots of prayers are answered like that. So be warned!

## *Problems Of Prayer*

If we start to pray from where we are in life and from what we are, all our problems will start to surface. Don't be mortified. It's good for them to be exposed – they are like wounds needing fresh air to heal.

Also don't be mortified for having problems. They are part of our human heritage. A joke dispels them, just as much as hours of kneework.

## *Pompousness*

A man is about to enter a place of worship, when he bumps into another man at the door.

"What are you asking God for?" he asks grandly.

"I'm asking Him for five pounds," says the other. "Life's really hard at the moment."

"Five pounds!" exclaims the first in disgust. "Why, I'm asking Him for five million to save my business empire."

An idea occurs to him. He takes out his wallet, peels off a fiver, and says: "Take this, my man, and don't bother Him or me." The second gasps and goes off with his fiver rejoicing.

The first man then makes his way into the empty place of worship, kneels down in a pew and starts to pray:

"Now, Lord, that I have Your undivided attention . . ."

When our own prayers get too pompous, it is useful to remember this one from the morning service:

What are we? What is our life? What is our love? What is our justice? What is our success? What is our endurance? What is our power? Lord our God, and God of our ancestors, what can we say before You, for in Your presence are not the powerful as nothing, the famous as if they have never existed, the learned as if without knowledge, and the intelligent as if without insight. Even the difference between people and animals is nothing.

God may prefer Fido to you!

## *Delusions Of Grandeur*

This story probably goes the rounds periodically in Jewish life, since in every generation someone or other believes that he might have been chosen to become the Messiah, and there are always followers to support his claims.

One great mystic in the last century visited Jerusalem where he met the Chief Rabbi of his country.

"Tell me," said the Chief Rabbi, "what's this I hear everyone saying, that you might be the Messiah? What makes you believe such a thing?"

"Ah," replied the mystic, with a modest bow, "I had a message from God telling me!"

"Funny," said the Chief Rabbi, "I don't remember sending such a message."

It's very easy to get caught up in delusions about our

importance and power, so prayer can help us gain a little detachment.

Lord, help me not take myself too seriously, for a lot of me is very funny; the games I get up to, the tricks I play, the fibs I tell myself, and the faces I make in life's mirror. I hope You enjoy them, Lord, even if I go beetroot with embarrassment when I remember them.

May they not be hurtful to others, just give them a giggle.

Thank you, Lord.

# *Day and Night*

## *Waking Up – A Little Resurrection*

As you rub your eyes and open them, say:

> Blessed are You, our Living God, Sovereign of the universe, who takes away sleep from my eyes and slumber from my eyelids.

As you sip your first cup of tea:

> Blessed are You, our Living God, Sovereign of the universe, by whose word all things exist.

Now remind yourself of your own goodness and the image of God within you.

> My God, the soul You have given me is pure, for You created it, You formed it and You made it live within me. You watch over it within me, but one day You will take it from me to everlasting life. My God and God of my ancestors, as long as the soul is within me, I will declare that You are the master of all deeds, the ruler of all creatures and the Lord of every soul. Blessed are You, Lord, who brings the dead into everlasting life.

As you think of the day ahead say:

> Help me to live according to Your teaching and to hold fast to Your commands. Let me not come into the power of sin or wrong-doing, temptation or disgrace. Let no evil within me control me; and keep me far from bad people and bad company. Help me hold fast to the good within me and to good deeds, and bend my will and my desires to serve You.

Now up you get and don't dive back under your duvet! Later during the day, you may experience odd flashes of insight. This may help to explain them.

> When a baby is about to be born, a light is held behind its head so that it can see all over the world. Then they teach it the entire Torah (God's teaching). But at the instant of birth an angel touches its mouth and it forgets everything. So all of life is spent remembering what we once knew.
>
> From the Talmud, Niddah

## *Dressing*

These blessings can be said as you wake up in the morning and dress, connecting each item of clothing with higher things.

*As you start to dress*

> Blessed are You, our Living God, Sovereign of the universe, who clothes those who are naked.

*As your morning stiffness starts to go*

> Blessed are You, our Living God, Sovereign of the universe, who frees those who are bound.

*As you try a tentative stretch*

Blessed are You, our Living God, Sovereign of the universe, who lifts up those bent low.

*As you put on socks and shoes*

Blessed are You, our Living God, Sovereign of the universe, who strengthens our steps.

*As you put on your belt or girdle*

Blessed are You, our Living God, Sovereign of the universe, who girds us with strength.

*As you adjust your hair, hairpiece or hat*

Blessed are You, our Living God, Sovereign of the universe, who crowns us with glory.

*As you get ready to face the day*

Blessed are You, our Living God, Sovereign of the universe, who gives strength to the weary.

Dressing up is fun and can be witty and wonderful. But don't let your outer packaging make you forget your inner self or soul.

*High heels*

God help me!
My head, I carry my head so high
no one I love can reach me.

God help me!
Wherever I go I see my slaves plodding
my loads laid on their bent necks,
my hand goes out to them, and I run after them
with my head up, on high heels.

God help me!
When I, I myself am so pale so thin
a little bread's enough for me and

a couple of yards would do
to wrap up this body –
why are so many backs
bowed beneath my loads?

Ah God, help my haughty head, and my high heels.

Malka Heifetz Tussman

## *Tying Knots*

Tie knots to remember, like knots in handkerchiefs. By saying these simple blessings, you connect the commonplaces of this life to eternity. Here are some traditional ones:

*On smelling flowers*
Blessed are You, our Living God, Sovereign of the universe, who creates fragrant plants.
*On smelling spices*
Blessed are You, our Living God, Sovereign of the universe, who creates different kinds of spices.
*On smelling perfumes*
Blessed are You, our Living God, Sovereign of the universe, who creates sweet-smelling oil.
*On seeing the wonders of nature*
Blessed are You, our Living God, Sovereign of the universe, who performs the work of creation.
*For thunder*
Blessed are You, our Living God, Sovereign of the universe, whose strength and power fill the world.
*On seeing a rainbow*
Blessed are You, our Living God, Sovereign of the

universe, who remembers Your covenant and is faithful to it, and keeps Your promise.

*On seeing the sea*

Blessed are You, our Living God, Sovereign of the universe, who made the great sea.

*On seeing the beauties of nature*

Blessed are You, our Living God, Sovereign of the universe, who has such as these in Your world.

*On seeing trees in blossom for the first time in the year*

Blessed are You, our Living God, Sovereign of the universe, who has not made Your world lack for anything and has created in it fine creatures and trees to give us pleasure.

*On hearing bad news*

Blessed are You, our Living God, Sovereign of the universe, the true judge.

*On hearing news which is good for you and for others*

Blessed are You, our Living God, Sovereign of the universe, who is good and does good.

*On seeing people of unusual appearance*

Blessed are You, our Living God, Sovereign of the universe, who varies the forms of creation.

Why not make up some of your own? – for example, when tasting a rare wine, or when drinking plonk, when giving up cigarettes or winning a premium bond.

A friend of mine waited for hours at the Coronation to say the blessing when sighting royalty. He missed the young Elizabeth, but got Queen Salote of Tonga instead and was mollified. If you move in royal circles, the blessing is:

Blessed are You, our Living God, Sovereign of the universe, who has given of Your glory to flesh and blood.

## *Going to Work*

It feels good to be part of a city as it wakes. There is a kinship of all workers. There is Tyburn Church near Marble Arch in London where early in the morning you can pray beside nightclub-goers and cleaners going home, and secretaries and store managers on their way to work.

If you've got any snobbism about particular kinds of work, then this prayer from the Talmud which is nearly two thousand years old deals with it nicely. The Rabbis at Yavneh were the Establishment of their faith, and the "bees knees", spiritually speaking.

The Rabbis of Yavneh used to say:
I was created by God and so is everyone else.
I work in the town and others work in the country.
I get up early to do my work and so do they.
They don't do my work, and I don't do theirs.
So how can you say, I do a lot and they do little?
It doesn't matter, provided it's done for the sake of heaven.

From the Talmud, Berachot

## *For Committee Meetings*

At committee meetings we put on special personalities. We raise points of order, we take umbrage, and generally get above ourselves. It is easy to get carried away by paper triumphs and defeats.

One way of bringing God into the committee involves no words. Select an empty chair, and, as it were, put God's presence in it. If you get carried away, glance at the chair, and be reminded of its invisible occupant.

This prayer is used at the start of committee meetings. If you don't know who Korach is, then look up your Bibles, Numbers 16. Hillel and Shammai were two early disputants in the Talmud, with different temperaments but both pious, and honourable, and, in their different ways, both right. If they don't mean much to you, substitute your own favourite godly antagonists.

> Let us come together in God's name and prepare ourselves to do His will. May His presence dwell among us, drawing us to serve Him and His creatures with justice and with love. Let us listen to each other with respect, and treat each other with wisdom and generosity, so that we witness to the Master whom we serve, and justify His choice of us. May none of our controversies rise up like those of Korach, from ambition and self-seeking. Let them only be for the sake of heaven, like those of Hillel and Shammai. May our eyes be open to see His greatness in the smallest things we do. Through our faithfulness may the cause of goodness prosper in the world.

## *In The Supermarket*

About nineteen hundred years ago, Rabbi Akiva compared life to what seems remarkably like a modern supermarket. The last sentence is extraordinarily reassuring.

> He used to say, Everything is given on pledge, and a net is spread for all living. The shop is open, and the shopkeeper gives credit, and the account is open and the hand writes, and whoever wishes to borrow may come and borrow. But the collectors go round every day, and exact payment from man with his consent or without it, and their claims are justified, and the judgment is a judgment of truth. Yet everything is prepared for the feast!
>
> Pirke Avot 3:20

Here is my own prayer:

Help me to be helpful in the supermarket, because that is where it all happens. I've seen people bumping others with their trolleys, or producing credit cards in the Cash Only queue or making life tough for the checkout girl. To be honest, I'm tempted to do all those things myself, but because of You, I won't. I want to be Your witness among the packets and bottles.

Help me to be helpful.

## *In The Launderette*

Wash me and I shall be whiter than snow.

Psalm 51:9

I watch my washing going round and round, and the dirt going out of it. It gives me a good feeling.
I suppose You watch us in the same way, hoping the dirt will come out of us.
I should like to be as clean as my clothes, so I shall
– offer a piece of my chocolate to the woman sitting next to me.
– not use foreign coins in the machines
– not pinch other people's hangers
– or leave puddles on the floor
– and help other people fold their sheets and tablecloths.
Wash me, Lord, I should like to be as clean as my clothes.

## *Kitchen*

Help me not hate my guests after they go and I face up to the washing up they leave behind.
Help me not attempt to make dishes that are too difficult for me so that I get annoyed with myself and uptight with my family. Cooking is for comfort and pleasure, not vanity.
Help me respect my tools and ingredients, and give them good vibes.
As I simmer my gravy and the flavours blend, help my jangled feelings blend in me. Cook me as I cook my ingredients. Lord, marinate me in Your grace.
Help me not to despise small things or get fed up when

my guests gobble up in five minutes the work of hours. Such unnoticed sacrifices keep the world going round. Help me make my kitchen friendly and comfortable. May I always find time to give friends who need them a friendly cuppa, some cake and some comfort and honest words with it.

Help me remember You are here with me in my kitchen. Perhaps I'll light a candle, or put a picture or text on the wall that reminds me of You. I can't cook for You but I won't forget You, even when I'm mixing, baking or frying. No, not frying . . . it's too dangerous.

## *As Daylight Fades*

The following prayers are said as the Day of Atonement service draws to an end at sunset, and we go home for our first food and drink after a day of fasting and prayer.

Twilight is a strange time when we are poised between day and night, wakefulness and sleep, this world and eternity.

You can adapt these words to your own feelings, omitting parts which don't feel relevant, as you make your way home when daylight fades.

> As daylight fades we pray for light. We remember the honest and the good, the lights that shine in our history. We remember the light that shines in everyone, and also in us. We recognize this light, and we know it – it is the light of goodness, it is God.
>
> As daylight fades we face the darkness in the world and the darkness that is in us too. The great

work waits for us at every moment, and calls to us. The starving need our food, the uncared for need our love, the rejected need our understanding. We need Your light so that we do not fail them nor leave them in darkness.

As daylight fades we turn to the darkness that lies within us – the hurts that never heal, the growths of bitterness or envy that time does not dissolve, the hatred that we can feel for others, the dislike we can feel for ourselves.

As daylight fades we look to that other time, seen in visions and known to prophets, when the sun of righteousness will arise for all Your creatures. Then all of us shall know that it is in giving that we find our contentment, in loving others that we ourselves find love, through forgiving others that we are forgiven, by blessing others that we ourselves are blessed.

As daylight fades Your promise to us is like a guiding star in the sky of night. "You shall be a blessing . . . and in you shall all the families of the earth be blessed." (Genesis 12:2–3)

## *Going Home From A Place Of Worship In The Evening*

The day is fading, the sun has set. Our father in heaven, quieten the doubts that rise within us, and our inner confusion, so that peace may find its way into our hearts and there make its home – Your peace which comes as we forgive others, and You forgive us.

Soon we shall journey from this house of prayer to our homes. May this peace we have sought here through our prayers and fasting return home with us, so that our homes can stand firm in life's storms, sheltering all that is generous and good in us from all that is mean and false.

For yet another home You have prepared for us, when our time on earth has ended: an eternal home more sure than all the earthly homes that we have known. The stars will soon appear in the dusk. Be our guiding star as we journey into life everlasting. And as the gates of this world close, open again the Gates of Mercy for us, and we shall enter in.

## *Undressing For Bed*

As you take your clothes off, fold them gently, and meditate or pray. As you put them away, try to put away with them any bitterness or bad feeling the day has left. You can, for example, make a parcel of all your frustrations and give them to God as a present! It's quite effective. You can also examine them in the light of eternity and what felt tragic can seem comic.

Try also to be at peace with your bedroom. Look at it as if you were an artist looking at a subject with its lights and shadows, like Rembrandt or Gwen John. Feel part of it.

In bed, it is a good time to read some poetry – it doesn't have to be pretentious.

Poems like this make God come close. George Herbert is very suitable too.

Lord, let Your light be only for the day,
And the darkness for the night.
And let my dress, my poor humble dress
Lie quietly over my chair at night.

Let the church-bells be silent,
My neighbour Ivan not ring them at night.
Let the wind not waken the children
Out of their sleep at night.

Let the hen sleep on its roost, the horse in the stable
All through the night.
Remove the stone from the middle of the road
That the thief may not stumble at night.

Let heaven be quiet during the night.
Restrain the lightning, silence the thunder,
They should not frighten mothers giving birth
To their babies at night.
And me too protect against fire and water,
Protect my poor roof at night.
Let my dress, my poor humble dress
Lie quietly over my chair at night.

Nachum Bomze

## *Before Going To Sleep*

Little prayers like these comfort and clear our minds. In some prayer books they are meant for children. They work just as well with adults.

Let me lie down in peace and rise again to a good life. Spread the covering of Your peace over me and protect me for such is Your being.

Into Your hands I entrust my spirit
and with my spirit, my body too.
You are with me, I shall not fear.

Blessed is my Creator by day and blessed by night. Blessed when He makes me lie down, and blessed when He wakes me up.

## *If You're Up To It*

The following prayer comes from the traditional prayer-book of the Sephardi Jews. The sentiments are the finest, but I must admit I'm not always fine enough to say it.

Master of the Universe, I now forgive and pardon anyone who made me angry or sinned against me – my person, my property, my honour or anything that is mine – whether by accident or design, intentionally or unintentionally, by word or deed, whether now or in a previous life. Let no one be punished because of me.

## *Prayers When You Wake Up At Night*

Think of all the people who are awake with you. Imagine them, say hello to them in your mind, and ask God to bless you and them together.

Lord I pray for
– nightclub hostesses
– nuns reciting psalms

– long-distance lorry drivers
– patients in hospital who can't sleep
– people who missed the last train
– parents woken up by babies.

I pray to You, O Lord
From all my heart,
O Lord! I pray to You
With fervour and zeal,
For the sufferings of the humiliated,
For the uncertainty of those who wait;
For the non-return of the dead;
For the helplessness of the dying;
For the sadness of the misunderstood,
For those who request in vain;
For all those abused, scorned and disdained;
For the silly, the wicked, the miserable;
For those who hurry in pain
To the nearest physician;
Those who return from work
With trembling and anguished hearts to their homes;
For those who are roughly treated and pushed aside,
For those who are hissed on the stage;
For all who are clumsy, ugly, tiresome and dull,
For the weak, the beaten, the oppressed,
For those who cannot find rest
During long sleepless nights;
For those who are afraid of Death,
For those who wait in pharmacies;
For those who have missed the train;
– For all the inhabitants of our earth
And all their pains and troubles,
Their worries, sufferings, disappointments,

All their griefs, afflictions, sorrows,
Longings, failures, defeats;
For everything which is not joy,
Comfort, happiness, bliss . . .
Let these shine for ever upon them
With tender love and brightness,
I pray to You O Lord most fervently –
I pray to You O Lord from the depths of my heart.

Juljan Tuwim

## *Life's Journey*

## *On A Journey*

In *Forms of Prayer* this is the blessing before going on a journey.

> May God who called our father Abraham to journey into the unknown, and guarded him, and blessed him, may He protect me too and bless my journey. May His confidence support me as I set out, may His spirit be with me on the way, and may He lead me back to my home in peace. Those I love, I commend to His care. He is with them, I shall not fear. As for myself, may His presence be my companion, so that blessing comes to me, and to everyone I meet.
>
> Blessed are You, Lord, whose presence journeys with His people.

I also sing a catchy number by Sidney Carter which begins:

"One more step along the world I go."

It's less stately but more suitable for a bus stop or a railway platform.

## *A New Home*

Unless the Lord builds the home its builders work in vain.

Psalm 127:1

As I enter my new home, I ask Your blessing on it and all those who live in it. May its doors be open to those in need and its rooms filled with tenderness. May love dwell within these walls, and joy shine from its windows. May Your peace protect it and Your presence dwell within it.
Thank You for bringing me to this happiness.

## *Before An Operation*

This is the conventional prayer:

> Before my operation I turn to You, because You are always beside me.
>
> You created the healing powers of my body and the strength and courage of my spirit. They are Your gifts to carry me from fear to confidence.
>
> Yours are the wonder of science and the marvel of creation. I thank You for the wisdom of my doctors, the skill of my surgeon's hands and the devotion of my nurses. They are Your helpers in the work of healing. They comfort me.
>
> Lord, I am Your child whom You created. Lead me gently into sleep and waken me to health. In Your love I trust.

If you are a fatalist with a black sense of humour, the following may express your feelings more accurately:

> Without your consent you were born, and without your consent you live, and without your consent you die, and without your consent you will have to give an account and a reckoning.
>
> Pirke Avot

So it's better to accept it and not think about it too much. Not being conscious, it's really a non-event.

## *Prayer On Behalf Of The Dangerously Ill*

*For a man*

I pray to You for my beloved . . . who approaches the frontiers of this life. You are the master over life and death and his fate is in Your hands. Heal his body and restore him to me, if this is Your will. If it is not, be with him where I cannot follow, and give him courage to conquer pain, and hope to overcome fear. Lead him forwards in peace from this world into the life that has no end, supported by his own good deeds, and accompanied by my love. Help me too, and teach me that though

*For a woman*

I pray to You for my beloved . . . who approaches the frontiers of this life. You are the master over life and death and her fate is in Your hands. Heal her body and restore her to me, if this is Your will. If it is not, be with her where I cannot follow, and give her courage to conquer pain, and hope to overcome fear. Lead her forwards in peace from this world into the life that has no end, supported by her own good deeds, and accompanied by my love. Help me too, and teach me that though we may part now, we shall come together once again in the gathering of life. His soul is in Your hand, and with his soul, his body too. You are with him, I shall not fear.

we may part now, we shall come together once again in the gathering of life. Her soul is in Your hand, and with her soul, her body too. You are with her, I shall not fear.

## *Growing Old*

Lord, the landscape of my life is changing – I am growing old. I can't cope with sleepless nights, nor two glasses of wine, and my waterworks are not what they were, which makes me feel ashamed and frightened. I've had to learn how to give up as well as give.

But I try to trust in You. As I pray I count my blessings, and thank you for freeing me from the burden of expectation others have laid upon me and I laid upon myself. I have also learnt to be more open and honest with You, which is a relief.

When I look back, I become irritable, but when I dare to look forward, I know that beyond the inevitable home, hospital or hospice that await me, I shall not die into the grave but into Your arms and into the gathering of life. I shall return home.

In the meantime help me to enjoy what each day brings and regard my own deficiencies and failures with humour. I shall try to do the same with others.

You are closer than before, and I am content.
Thank You, Lord!

## *Approaching Death*

We are all approaching it, of course, but to some it seems nearer than to others. Falling asleep is a sort of dress rehearsal. The old-style poetess Alice Lucas took it rather sadly.

Lord, I am weary, yet I dare not pray
That Thou wilt ease me of my load.
At Thy command I bear it all the day,
And Thou hast traced my road.

Lord, I am fearful of the shades of night,
That darkening o'er my path descend.
Yet vain it were to pray for lengthening light,
That I my task may end.

Lord, I am troubled, yet I will not plead
With Thee for days of happiness,
While all around I see my brethren's need,
Their anguish and distress.

Lord, be it so! I will not ask of Thee
To give me rest from toil and care,
Or length of days, but this alone shall be
My heart's unceasing prayer.

Lord, grant to me, nor yet to me alone,
But unto all on earth who dwell,
Faith that Thy love, through ways to us unknown,
Doth order all things well.

Lord, grant us faith, then, though we work and weep,
Thy peace will guard us on our way,
And we shall lay us down in peace, and sleep
When comes the close of day.

Alice Lucas

Dying, some say, is pleasant, and some even say ecstatic. This may be true as we shall meet at long last the Being we've only glimpsed in prayer.

## *Before A Funeral*

*For a man*

Merciful Father, be with us as we gather in this house, the home of our dear one who has gone forward to life everlasting. We remember all his goodness. May his memory be a blessing.

Help us to remember that the soul does not die, and our dear one has gone to that eternal home which You prepared for us when our work on earth is done, and our time here has ended. Open the gates of mercy for him. May he enter into everlasting peace. In Your light we see beyond the frontiers of death to the life that has no end.

*For a woman*

Merciful Father, be with us as we gather in this house, the home of our dear one who has gone forward to life everlasting. We remember all her goodness. May her memory be a blessing.

Help us to remember that the soul does not die, and our dear one has gone to that eternal home which You prepared for us when our work on earth is done, and our time here has ended. Open the gates of mercy for her. May she enter into everlasting peace. In Your light we see beyond the frontiers of death to the life that has no end.

This house was built by human hands, but we shall come together in a home where we shall never part, surrounded by Your presence. Amen.

## *Remembering Someone Who Died*

After a candle of remembrance is lit, say:

"The memory of the righteous is as a blessing."

*For a man*

Today I remember with love . . . who has gone to everlasting life, and I honour his memory. As this light burns pure and clear, so may the thought of his goodness shine in my heart and strengthen me, Lord, to do Your will. Amen.

God full of compassion whose presence is over us, grant perfect rest beneath the shelter of Your presence with the holy and pure on high who shine as the lights of heaven, to . . . who has gone to his everlasting home. Master of mercy, cover him in the shelter of Your wings for ever, and bind his soul into the gathering of life. It is the Lord who is

*For a woman*

Today I remember with love . . . who has gone to everlasting life, and I honour her memory. As this light burns pure and clear,, so may the thought of her goodness shine in my heart and strengthen me, Lord, to do Your will. Amen.

God full of compassion whose presence is over us, grant perfect rest beneath the shelter of Your presence with the holy and pure on high who shine as the lights of heaven, to . . . who has gone to her everlasting home. Master of mercy, cover her in the shelter of Your wings for ever, and bind her soul into the gathering of life. It is the Lord who is

*For a man*

his heritage. May he be at peace in his place of rest. Amen.

*For a woman*

her heritage. May she be at peace in her place of rest. Amen.

# *Relationships*

## *Falling In Love With Love*

Where I wander – You!
Where I ponder – You!
Only You, You again, always You!
You! You! You!
When I am gladdened – You!
When I am saddened – You!
Only You, You again, always You!
You! You! You!
Sky is You, earth is You!
You above! You below!
In every trend, at every end,
Only You, You again, always You!
You! You! You!

Levi Yitzchak of Berditchev

O God, I don't want Your paradise; I don't want the joy of the next world; I only want You Yourself.

Shneur Zalman of Ladi

Loving God and loving a human being are not that different. It's the level and purity of love that makes the difference. In the sayings of the Fathers (an early bit of the Talmud) it says:

If love depends on some selfish cause when the cause disappears love disappears; but if love does not depend on a selfish cause it will never disappear. What love depended on a selfish cause? Amnon's love for Tamar (2 Samuel 13). What love did not depend on a selfish cause? David's love for Jonathan (1 Samuel 18).

Pirke Avot 5:19

You can therefore pray to God with any popular love song, by dedicating it to Him or Her or It. But do remember God is spirit, so use the erotic impulse sparingly.

## *Anyone To Anyone In Love*

Sing together, holding hands, any popular love song. Or recite any selection from the biblical Song of Songs – though be warned, it's powerful stuff. I remember a reading of a new translation at a club. He was a chubby young accountant with glasses, she was plain and rather blue-stockingish, so it all seemed rather comical. Two chapters into the reading, the two speakers were crimson and the atmosphere electric.

I slept, but my heart was awake.
Listen, my beloved is knocking.
"Open to me, my sister, my love,
my dove, my perfect one;
for my head is wet with dew,
my locks with the drops of the night."
I had put off my garment,
how could I put it on?
I had bathed my feet,
how could I soil them?

My beloved put his hand to the latch,
and my heart was thrilled within me.
I arose to open to my beloved,
and my hands dripped with myrrh,
my fingers with liquid myrrh,
upon the handles of the bolt.

Song of Songs 5:2–5

Or from the closing chapter:

Set me as a seal upon your heart,
as a seal upon your arm;
for love is strong as death,
passion as cruel as the grave.

Even if you giggle, love needs a celebration and if it's real love, the unselfish not the manipulative kind, God is in it somewhere.

Many religious lovers feel they ought to pray together. Apart from one or two unplanned occasions, I personally find it too embarrassing. Private prayer is very private – like taking a bath.

## *An Engagement*

A marriage even! In the morning before breakfast, some people make "marriage rings" round their fingers with leather straps. They are engaging themselves to God.

As they make the "rings", they say these words of Hosea who knew a lot about love, both the human and the divine sort.

I betroth you to me for ever.
I betroth you to me with integrity and justice,
with tenderness and love.
I betroth you to me with faithfulness
and you will know the Lord.

Hosea 2:21–22

You can also do it mentally, but remember God is not just another bigger being, but something quite different which will check any gushing or over-the-top emotionalism.

## *A Man To A Woman*

It is nice to say something nice to your spouse/partner/significant other/the only one who understands you, etc.

Traditionally a husband recited this chapter of the Book of Proverbs to his wife at the Sabbath Eve meal. It comes of course from another age, so it may sound sexist – but she might like it. Try it out – but omit the verses that don't apply.

A woman of worth, who can find her?
for she is more precious than rubies.
Her husband trusts her in his heart
and has no loss by it.
Every day of her life
she does him good, not harm.
Her hand is held out open to the poor,
reaching out to those in need.
She is clothed in strength and dignity,
serene before the time to come.

When she speaks, it is with wisdom
  and on her tongue is the guidance of love.
She looks after her home with care,
  and does not idle away her time.
Her children stand up and honour her,
  and her husband sings her praises.
"Many a woman has done splendid deeds,
  but you surpass them all."
Charm deceives and beauty fades,
  so praise the woman who honours God.
Give her honour for the work of her hands,
  and her own good deeds will praise her in public.

From Proverbs 31

## *A Woman To A Man*

This is the return match – not so traditional, of course. Again, omit the bits that don't apply.

Praise the Lord!
  Happy the man who fears the Lord,
  who takes great joy in His commands.
His children will be powerful on earth,
  an upright generation are well blessed.
Wealth and prosperity are in his house,
  his righteous deeds stand firm for ever.
He is a light in darkness for the upright,
  he is generous, merciful and just.
It is good when a man is generous and lends
  and conducts his affairs with honour.
For a righteous man will never waver
  and he will be remembered for ever.

He does not fear bad news,
his heart is firm, he trusts in the Lord.
His heart is steadfast, he does not fear,
he will see the downfall of his foes.
He is open-hearted, he gives to the poor;
his righteousness stands firm for ever,
his head held high with honour.

From Psalm 112

## *Making Love*

**Before**

The physical side of love is part of a human relationship. There is even a law that forbids a man to say his evening prayers on his wedding night – since his mind won't really be on the job! And part of the celebration of the Sabbath, to experience its joy, is to make love on Friday night with your spouse.

It may not be a time for conscious prayers, but they're present in our minds, nevertheless. They may not be very pious, but they're no less sincere.

Dear God, this is awfully important, please help me get it right!

Excuse me for a moment, God, but I really need this release.

Thank You for letting us share each other in this way.

Help me make it work for him/her!

Heigh ho, duty calls!

How comfortable we are with each other, God; thank You for our companionship and love.

**And After**

God, that was wonderful! Let's do it again!

Is that all there is? We were one for a moment, but I'm still me. Is that the difference, God, between love and passion? Help me value the highs and accept the lows.

That was fun, God, we enjoyed each other. Thank You!

Dear God, I really botched that up! The physical side I can't do much about, but maybe I should be a little more caring and learn what he/she needs. Help us learn to understand each other better.

How nice to be quiet together, and share a silence. Or talk honestly, without pretences. I wish it could always be like this, God. Amen.

## *For Friends*

In a modern city, one's friends are one's family. As other relationships have become more fluid, flexible or non-existent, friendship has become more important. Yet there is no service in traditional liturgies to celebrate it and very few prayers. Though it is true that the most moving words in the Bible are said by David over Jonathan (2 Samuel 1:17–27), and by Ruth to Naomi (Ruth 1:16–17).

> Lord, I want to thank You for my friends who, over the years, like You, have come to know what I am, and still put up with me. We won't become one flesh or anything like that, and we probably don't agree on that much either and we're not going to change.

But we have learnt to accept each other as we are, and prefer each other like that.

## *A Prayer For Animals*

The Bible shows great concern for the animal world – animals that will harm each other should not be harnessed together; working animals should rest on the Sabbath; they should be fed before their master. The tradition is picked up by the Rabbis as this story shows:

Rabbi Judah the Prince was studying Torah when a calf passed before him on its way to slaughter. It began to cry as if pleading to be saved. Rabbi Judah said: "What can I do for you, you were fashioned for this purpose!" As a punishment for being so heartless he suffered toothache for thirteen years. He was only relieved of it when he prevented his daughter killing a weasel, quoting the words from the Psalm: "God's mercies are over all His works."

Genesis Rabbah 33:3

Nearly a thousand years ago, Maimonides taught about blood sports:

We should not kill animals for the purpose of practising cruelty, or for the purpose of play.

I once inserted the names of my dogs in the list read out before Memorial prayers. There were one or two protests but most understood the depth of love that can bind beasts and human beings. For me it was dogs. For some it is cats, and some like talking to cows, who are always sympathetic in their sad, shy, muzzy way.

> Lord, I remember my poor pooches, Re'ach and Djilas (please insert your own names) who have now gone to whatever place You have appointed for big, black dogs. I only ask it be near the place You have appointed for me. Through them I learnt companionship and loyalty and the ecstasy of snow, sticks and sky. I thank You for lending them to my care. I am sorry for any harm I did them and when my turn comes to leave this life I only ask that You will be as forgiving to me as they were, and bind us together into the gathering of life.

## *For Machinery*

I've never been good with my hands and any kind of machine is potentially disastrous. Struggling with a word processor was the first time I felt I had a machine I could at least reason with, and figuring out its tricks was like playing chess with a precocious six-year-old.

Cars are another matter. They encourage intimacy and private chats and encouragement, especially on long trips alone. "Well done, old dear, we made it home again!" "Thanks for starting first time!" It's partly magic and partly to appease, since so many mysterious things can go wrong. This extract from a poem by Barry Holtz sums up a whole world of experience.

She never seemed quite at home in the world,
Technology amazed her, and she would spend her
Days staring out the window of her apartment,
Trying, it seemed, to comprehend it all. "What
Does she do all day," I asked my mother. "She
Counts the cars," my mother replied, as if this
Were a proper activity for an elderly woman,
A simple strategy to order things not understood.

A pious woman, she was unknowingly an animist,
A technological mystic who believed in the souls
Of things. As when our car was stopped at a traffic
Light one day and we fumed, late for some appointment,
She suggested that it was good,
For after all cars too needed to take a rest.

Since tradition talks of "the miracles that are daily with us" perhaps this blessing is appropriate when any bit of machinery actually works:

> Blessed are You, our Living God, Sovereign of the universe, who performed a wonderful thing for me at this place.

One Rabbi reformulated the 23rd Psalm as:
The Lord is my bus driver, I shall not crash.

# *Rituals*

## *Lighting a Candle . . .*

Lighting candles brings the presence of God very close. Candles are lit for Sabbaths and festivals, and to remember relations and friends who have died. They also give "atmosphere" to secular occasions like parties and the tables of those who dine alone. Lighting a candle can be a prayer.

Here is a prayer which is said after lighting Sabbath candles. You can adapt it to your own needs. Make it personal by saying "me" instead of "us", and your own community and special occasion in place of Israel and the Sabbath. Prayers grow. They are not to be pickled and preserved, but used.

> God of might, light of the world, bless us with a perfect blessing in Your presence. Enlighten our eyes with Your light and Your truth, just as we light the Sabbath candles before You, and so make a spirit of trust and love dwell in our homes. Guide us with the light of Your presence, for in Your light we see light. Send Your blessing to every home of Israel and to the whole world, and set peace and eternal blessing upon them. Amen.

## *A Prayer For The Day Of Rest*

The greatest biblical invention was the Sabbath, a regular day of rest for everybody, animals included. Work is not the climax of creation but what we are working for.

To find out what that is, you need to rest yourself. At first real rest can seem uncomfortable – rather like prayer, but gradually as you get used to the quietness and silence, something in you turns inside out and you almost cry with relief.

Here is a meditation of Reform Jews, which concerns the Sabbath.*

> God, I prepare to honour my day of rest, keeping faith with You and the generations that have gone before. I cast away any hatred or bitterness that lingers from the week that is past, so that my spirit may be at rest, and I can truly speak Your name. I see those about me in the light of these candles as You want me to see them, and thank You for family and friendship, loyalty and love. I make the blessing over wine and receive the gift of happiness, the peace that comes from holiness, the joy that comes from giving. As I eat my meal, I remember all I owe to others, and look forward to the time when all shall find their joy and peace.

*I have adapted it for any day of rest.

## *For An Anniversary*

You are our Creator and our remembrance is always before You, though times pass and seasons change according to Your plan. Today I come before You with my private memories, and thank You for my experience of companionship and love.

Whatever the future brings, may this day strengthen me and renew me on my journey through life. I thank You in my heart for the happiness and kindness I have known. Bless me in the years that lie ahead.

## *Grace After Meals*

The Bible says: "You shall eat and be satisfied and bless the Lord, your God" (Deuteronomy 8:10), which means that the main grace is said *after* you have eaten and been satisfied, not before.

The traditional grace is long and formal and not meant for fast food. It begins:

> Blessed are You, Our Living God, Sovereign of the universe, who feeds the whole world through Your goodness, with grace, kindness and mercy. You give food to all flesh, for Your love is for ever. Through Your great goodness food has never failed us, and may it never fail us because of Your greatness; for You feed and provide for all and do good to all, and prepare food for all Your creatures that You have created. Blessed are You, Lord, who gives food to all.

And nearer the end come these simple prayers which can be used at many times of life, not just after food. The Hebrew for "All-merciful" is "Harachaman" ("ch" as in the Scottish "loch"). It is often chanted over and over again to all sorts of melodies, sacred and secular, such as "John Brown's Body", "The Student Prince", and the "Hymn To Joy" from Beethoven's Ninth.

The All-merciful, may You rule over us for ever and ever.
The All-merciful, may You be blessed in heaven and on earth.
The All-merciful, may You be praised through all generations, glorified among us for eternity, and honoured among us for ever.
The All-merciful, may You give us an honourable livelihood.
The All-merciful, may You send a plentiful blessing on this house, and on this table at which we have eaten.
The All-merciful, may You send Elijah the prophet – may he be remembered for good! – who will bring us good news of salvation and comfort.
The All-merciful, may You bless all who are seated here, us and all that is ours, as our fathers Abraham, Isaac and Jacob, and our mothers Sarah, Rebeccah, Rachel and Leah were each of them blessed with "everything". So may You bless all of us together with a perfect blessing. Amen.
The All-merciful, may You make us worthy of the messianic days and the life of the world to come.

Every district has, of course, its own forms of Grace. In Lancashire I was told people say:

"May we who are sinners
deserve our dinners."

Which puts it all in a nutshell.

Some Christians say

"For bacon and for buttered toast
praise Father, Son and Holy Ghost."

Alas it is impossible to Judaize it without sacrificing both rhyme and content.

Why not make your own?

## *Confession*

We try to confess our sins to God, and yet our confessions are formal or fake. A private confession before the Public Confession can clear the ground. This exercise gives some clue as to what might go wrong. It was written for the Day of Atonement, but can be adapted easily.

> Lord, I do not want to pester or repeat again or chant my list of sins once more. You knew the list before this day began. I recited them more for myself than for You. In fact, You know those which are still unknown to me, sins which I hid from myself or was too stupid to see.
>
> I confess that I have been responsible for much that went wrong. I tried to get more out of life than I

was willing to put into it. I never learnt to ask the right question. I did not say "What can I give life?" but "What can life give me?" Perhaps I cheated others. I certainly cheated myself of many things I could have had – friendship, love and self-respect.

I confess that a lot of my troubles came because I did not want to know the truths about myself or my life. I tried to buy what cannot be bought. I looked for permanence in passing things. I followed the crowd because I did not have the courage to stand alone.

And I also confess that I let my knowledge of You fade away. Many hopes and visions died because I did not trust them, though they were the signs of Your presence in my life.

I have stumbled through so many prayers today, and uttered so many words that I have lost touch with much of their meaning. I am bewildered by their certainties and their demands. Let this confession at least be true and my own prayer.

For I confess that many confessions I made were not quite true. I blamed myself for the wrong things. I mentioned my failings but not my sins. I tried to pretend I was someone else, not the person You created.

I am too small to reach You and You are too great for me to comprehend. Therefore I shall try to be still, and in the stillness wait patiently for You to find me. You are so great, You can bend down to me, and the distance between us which my mind could not cover, Your love can bridge.

Forgive me, pardon me, and grant me atonement.

# *Life's Meaning*

## *Pockets*

This prayer is based on the teaching of a great Chasidic master, Rabbi Bunam of Pshysha:

> God, I am the kind of person who keeps his hands in his pockets. In my right pocket I have, as it were, a slip of paper with the words: "You created the entire world just for my sake!" In the left there is another slip of paper, as it were, which says: "I am a fleeting cloud, a passing shadow, just dust and ashes."
>
> When I put my hands in my pockets, help me to remember the messages they contain, for today I shall need to remember them both.

## *Today*

Rabbi Joshua met the prophet Elijah at the mouth of the cave of Rabbi Simeon ben Yochai.

"When is the Messiah coming?" he asked.

"Go and ask him yourself," replied Elijah.

"But where shall I find him?"

"In front of the gates of Rome."

"How shall I be able to recognize him?"

"He is sitting among poor people covered with wounds. The others unbind all their wounds at the same time and then bind them all up again. But he only unbinds one wound at a time, and then binds it up immediately.

"He tells himself: 'Perhaps I shall be needed (to appear as the Messiah) – and I must not delay and arrive late!'"

So Rabbi Joshua travelled to Rome and found him. "Peace be with you, my master and teacher," he said.

He replied: "Peace be with you, son of Levi!"

The Rabbi Joshua asked: "Master, when are you coming?"

He answered, "Today!"

He went back to Elijah and said: "He deceived me, he deceived me! He told me, 'Today I am coming!' but he has not come."

But Elijah replied: "This is what he actually said: 'Today – if you would only hear God's voice.'" (Psalm 95:7).

From the Talmud, Sanhedrin

It's an important story. Waiting for someone else to come down and put your world to rights is a child's dream.

Rabbi Yochanan ben Zakkai used to say: If they tell you the Messiah's come when you are holding a plant in your hand, first plant it and only then go out to meet him.

Avot d'Rabbi Natan

It's better to look for the bit of Messiah in you, and when you've located it, give it some practice.

> Our holiest duty is to cherish the Messianic spark in our soul and make sure it's never extinguished.
>
> Nachman of Bratzlav

When you get up in the morning say to yourself:

> Lord, I should like to be of service to someone today. I'd like to be a Messiah to a person or an animal. When the opportunity comes, help me to notice it.

Before you go to sleep at night think over the day and see if you were a bit of someone's Messiah. Sometimes you don't realize it at the time. If you have, it's a true feeling, and you can repeat the Messiah experience tomorrow.

## *Ordinary People*

You didn't reveal Yourself to angels but to ordinary people like me. So don't let perfectionism put me off, or snobbish sermons defeat me before I begin. You know what I am and where I am in life and what my possibilities are. Help me today to do a little bit more than I normally would, and take one step farther than it is comfortable to go. I try to see Your image in the people I want to help, because even if I don't like them, I love You.

Amen

## *Gratitude*

Counting your blessings.

Why depress God consistently with your sins? Why not cheer Him up with your successes?

When I feel low, I sometimes count my blessings, and thank God for them one by one. I recommend the exercise.

Here are some of my own "Thank You's":

Thank You
- for having survived.
- for being born in England and not experiencing the Holocaust.
- for being a Rabbi – I've enjoyed it.
- for comfort food, like fruit pies and cold custard.
- for a friendly cup of tea.
- for my body – I've enjoyed that too.
- for the BBC World Service that I listen to late at night.
- for helping me make up after rows.
- for . . .

You can fill in the rest yourself!

## *Charity*

There are eight degrees in the giving of charity, one higher than the other:

> Those who give grudgingly, reluctantly, or with regret.
>
> Those who give less than they should, but give graciously.

> Those who give what they should, but only after they are asked.
> Those who give before they are asked.
> Those who give without knowing to whom they give, although the recipient knows the identity of the donor.
> Those who give without making their identity known.
> Those who give without knowing to whom they give, and the recipient not knowing the identity of the donor.
> Those who help people to support themselves by a gift, or a loan, or by finding employment for them, thus helping them to become self-supporting.
>
> Maimonides

There is a whole hierarchy of charities and a library of books on the subject. Maimonides's eight grades are a useful checklist – as relevant now as they were nearly a thousand years ago. But the important thing is to get started. Once you get started, you find giving is addictive. The pleasure is two-way, which is sane and right.

It deepens when you give some thinking as well as a coin. In fact, coins are not usually the best thing to give beggars. Food such as sandwiches and chocolate are better. If you continue giving, you end up by giving a bit of what you are as well as what you have.

But don't be put off by all this. Doing charity is better than defining it.

These words are similar to those of St Francis. They can help strengthen our will:

It is in giving that we find contentment, in serving that we find our true freedom and in blessing others that we ourselves are blessed.

But what you give is the real prayer, especially if it's a sacrifice. It affirms that there is something higher than yourself and what you want. The Bible says: "Love the Lord your God with all your heart, with all your soul and with all your might." The Rabbis asked, what is the meaning of "might"? One of them answered: "It means, with all your money!"

## *Being Human And Making Mistakes*

However close I think I get to You, help me to remember that I am not You and can never be You.

Though You made me in Your image and gave me freedom, I am still Your creature. I make mistakes, I do things wrong, I say things wrong, I know how to live just when I'm past it, it's like running after a moving bus.

But before I get annoyed with myself and angry, I remember You made me as You wanted me. Making mistakes is my business, my occupation. We can't help making them when we're trying to put our souls and body together, in this world and the next.

It's like trying to cover a table with a cloth that's too small. You get one end covered, and the other doesn't fit. You feel a fool.

Still, Lord, that's the way You created me. And I don't

mind making mistakes, if that's the way You want it. I'm only human – who knows that better than You?

Amen (optional)

## *Helping God To Help You*

Izzy prays in Synagogue:

"O, Lord, I've never asked You for anything before. But times are hard, so can I please have a win on the premium bonds?" No answer came from on high.

Izzy visits the Synagogue the following week.

"Lord," he prays, "I haven't heard from You. Have You forgotten me? I only wanted a small win on the premium bonds." Again no answer came from on high.

Izzy visits the Synagogue for a third time.

"Lord," he prays sadly, "I think You've really forgotten me, and I only wanted a small win on the premium bonds."

But this time a voice does come from heaven and it says, "Izzy, my child, can't you help me a little too? Can't you at least buy one premium bond?"

There is always a tension within religious people between acting ourselves and leaving things to God. Bar Kochba, a military leader, who some thought was the Messiah, led the Jewish revolt against Rome in the first century. Before going into battle he used to say: "O Lord, help neither us nor our enemy!"

Lots of prayers remind us of how much we are dependent on God. This simple prayer, from the end of the Book of Lamentations, suggests that it has to be a two-way traffic:

Lord, bring us back to You, and we shall return.

Lamentations 5:21

## *Doubting God And His Providence*

An older colleague, now dead, who was one of my teachers, wrote this prayer (this is a modernized version).

Lord, I have not always been true to You in my thoughts. I have doubted Your goodness, Your justice and Your very existence. The pressures of life were too strong, its bitterness more than I could bear. Everything went wrong with my hopes and my plans, and there seemed no way out, no way to turn. I said, "There is no justice in this life of ours!" Sometimes my own suffering, but still more the suffering of others, strengthened my doubts. "Why," I asked, "does God make His own children suffer? Where is His love? Where is His power?" At this point, You almost ceased to exist for me. Your hand would have held me, guided me, comforted me, but I lost touch with You. I should have looked for You more steadily, searched for You more diligently.

Out of my limited experience and my small knowledge, I judged the source of justice, and set my cleverness higher than the ultimate wisdom. I saw only one side of truth – the darkness, not the light. I forgot the smiling face of life and its beauty. I also forgot that the pain of life itself can lead to

> deeper compassion, and is a teacher of great wisdom. Because I was proud, and claimed to understand what was beyond me, I did not see that human goodness is a token of its creator's goodness.
>
> Pardon my conceit and my blindness. Help me to greater detachment so that I may see with greater steadiness and calm. Help me to find order in the apparent chaos of human life, and love even in its defeats and trials. Your mercy is always there: You know and feel our pain. Amen.

Belonging to a later generation, I don't regard doubt in such a negative light. It too is divine and the prelude to new faith. It is uncomfortable of course like birth pangs. If you doubt, don't be dishonest about it or you'll become a danger to yourself and others. Accept your doubt as a gift of God. He just wants you to move on.

Yes, it's religiously comfortable where you are and you don't want to move on.

But religion is about truth not cosiness. Sorry!

## *Fear*

My grandparents wore amulets protecting them against the "evil eye" and whatever else they feared, which was a lot as they lived in a spirit-haunted world. They wore little cases of metal or wood which contained comforting verses from the Psalms. The cases are no longer worn, but the words can still be helpful. If you are afraid, say any of the following:

Though a thousand may fall at your side,
ten thousand at your right hand
no harm can come to you.

Psalm 91:7

We are afraid of things that cannot harm us, and we know it. And we long for things that cannot help us, and we know it. But actually it is something within us that we are afraid of, and it is something within us that we long for.

Chasidic

Do not be afraid, for I am with you.

Genesis 26:24

Though I walk through the valley of the shadow of death
I fear no harm
for You are beside me.
Your rod and staff
they comfort me.

Psalm 23:4

The Lord is my light and my safety;
whom shall I fear?

Psalm 27:1

## *A Simple Meditation*

My God, keep my tongue from causing harm and my lips from telling lies. Let me be silent if people curse me, my soul still humble and at peace with all. Open my heart to Your teaching, and give me the

> will to practise it. May the plans and schemes of those who seek my harm come to nothing. May the words of my mouth and the meditation of my heart be acceptable to You, O Lord, my rock and my redeemer.

This simple meditation, said silently, concludes the "Standing Prayer", the heart of the liturgy. It was probably written by Mar bar Ravina in the fourth century of the Common Era (AD). It says what has to be said by a religious person, without frills. It is useful to recite during the day between appointments.

## *The Evil Impulse*

The evil impulse must be understood, not just condemned. It may be the unloved part in us, good that runs backwards on itself.

These passages are good to meditate on in a quiet few minutes in an empty synagogue, church or other place of worship. The experiences they describe are universal and recognizable to everyone. Before you pray, sit down and recognize them. Then you won't be caught by surprise.

> "And God saw everything that He had made and, behold, it was very good" (Genesis 1:31). This refers to the two impulses in people, the good impulse and the impulse to evil. But is the impulse to evil "very good"? "If it were not for that impulse,

people would not build houses, marry, have children or businesses."

Genesis Rabbah

The impulse to evil does not walk along the pavement but along the middle of the road. When it sees a man ogling with his eyes, straightening his hair and swaggering, it says "This one is mine!"

Genesis Rabbah

The impulse to evil is like someone who runs about the world with his hand closed. Nobody knows what's inside it. He asks: "What do you suppose I have in my hand?" And everyone thinks that what he wants most is hidden there. So they run after the impulse to evil. Then he opens his hand and there is nothing there.

Chasidic

In the next world God will slay the impulse to evil in the presence of both the righteous and wicked. To the righteous it will seem like a mountain, but to the wicked like a hair. Both will cry. The righteous will sob: "How did we overcome such a lofty mountain?" The wicked will sob: "Why weren't we able to overcome a single hair like this?"

From the Talmud, Succah

## *God Is Our Refuge*

Do not rely on God changing the universe to suit your convenience. As I said before, think of all the prayers that were said on the way to the concentration camps.

Prayer doesn't give us worldly security but it can give us courage and even if we lose our body, we don't have to lose our soul. In this sense God is our refuge. Prayer also opens up possibilities in a situation that we just didn't notice, or didn't want to see.

These verses from the Psalms are good steadiers when the going gets rough.

> Take pity on me, God, take pity,
> for in You my soul has taken refuge.
> I take refuge in the shadow of Your wings
> until the storms are past.
>
> Psalm 57:1

> Out of the depths I called to You, O God,
> God, hear my voice.
> Let Your ears listen
> to the voice of my pleading . . .
>
> I hope in God,
> my soul has hope,
> and for God's word I wait.
> My soul waits for God
> more than watchmen for the morning,
> watching for the morning.
>
> Psalm 130:1–2, 5–6

I lift up my eyes to the hills,
where shall I find my help?
My help is from God alone,
maker of heaven and earth.

Psalm 121:1–2

God, you are my God,
with longing do I seek You.
My soul is thirsty for You,
my flesh is pining for You
in a dry and weary land
where there is no water.

Psalm 63:1

## *Getting Rid Of Bad Memories*

Bad memories, old guilts, festering anger – we carry huge chunks of our past along with us. Some of it can only be worked through by years of therapy. Can prayer be of help in lightening the burden?

In ancient Israel they used to confess their sins once a year, try to make amends to each other, then sent all the unresolved bits and pieces into the wilderness on the back of a goat. If the ritual of the "scapegoat" was powerful enough, it must have given them a great sense of relief.

When the Temple fell and the ceremony was stopped (which was better for the poor goat), some resourceful person came up with a ceremony called "Tashlich", which means something like "chucking away". At the New Year period, people go to the sea or the nearest river or stream, and empty out the dust of their pockets or throw breadcrumbs into the water. Again they've had to do the personal homework and repair any special damage first, but this way they can add a symbolic cleansing and watch their personal rubbish float away.

You might like to try it by a stream near you. The words that belong to the ceremony come from the prophet Micah (Micah 7:19), "and You will cast all their sins into the depths of the sea."

It is no substitute for the work of purification on oneself, but it may help you finish the process, once and for all.

N.B. Be careful what you cast into a stream or the sea. Pollution is also a sin.

# *God*

## *Where Is God?*

A retreat I went to had this for its title, and it stays in my mind:

God is nowhere!
God is now here!

In prayer you can pass from one to the other in the twinkling of an eye. To the mind God may seem as distant as in this prayer:

> What can we say before You – so distant is the place where You are found? And what can we tell You – Your being is remote as the heavens? Yet You know everything, hidden and revealed. You know the mysteries of the universe and the intimate secrets of everyone alive. You probe our body's state, You see into the heart and mind. Nothing escapes You, nothing is hidden from Your gaze.

But in experience He can be very close, as in this story:

> "Where is the dwelling of God?"
>
> This is the question with which the Rabbi of Kotzk surprised a number of learned men who happened to be visiting him.
>
> They laughed at him: "What a thing to ask! Is not the whole world full of His glory?"

Then he answered his own question:
"God dwells wherever man lets Him in."

Martin Buber

## *Who Or What Is God?*

Who or What is the object of prayer, its purpose and its reason? Intellectually all paths of rational enquiry lead to paradox. But in living, this paradox becomes so close, so loving, so intimate, so concerned, rational people even the shrewd and worldly-wise stake their lives on it – and it supports them.

Here are some of the testimonies from the past – scattered through prayerbooks – which attempt to describe what is beyond description:

> "I am that I am." (Exodus 3:14)
> "The Lord, the Lord, a God of mercy and compassion, slow to anger, generous in love and truth, showing love to thousands, forgiving sin, wrong and failure; who pardons." (Exodus 34:6–7)

This hymn describes two perceptions of God – distant, remote, "transcendent", and loving, intimate, "immanent". They are contrasting in concept, but unified in our experience.

Eternal God who ruled alone
before creation of all forms,
at whose desire all began
and as the Sovereign was proclaimed.

Who after everything shall end
alone, in awe, will ever reign,
who was and is for evermore,
the glory that will never change.

Unique and One, no other is
to be compared, to stand beside,
neither before nor following,
alone the source of power and might.

This is my God, who saves my life,
the rock I grasp in deep despair,
the flag I wave, the place I hide,
who shares my cup the day I call.

In my Maker's hand I lay my soul
both when I sleep and when I wake,
and with my soul my body too,
my God is close, I shall not fear.

## *A Conversation With God*

Quite often an inner conversation develops into a prayer, and a prayer into an inner conversation between you and God. Don't get worried or feel you're going nuts, lots of people share the experience . . . Be wary though, if you can't easily distinguish fantasy and reality.

With that warning, on you go.

A lot of your own mental fluff gets mixed up in the

"conversation", but using your common sense, it eventually settles down. Over the course of time you'll find out if it helps you to heaven or just to cloud-cuckoo-land.

Here are some examples from well-thought-of religious figures who also had chats with the Almighty:

Cain had to learn from God what it meant to have killed his brother Abel – he couldn't just dismiss what he'd done saying: "Am I my brother's keeper?" (Genesis 4:8–10).

Rebecca learnt from God about why she was having such a difficult pregnancy (Genesis 25:19–24).

Jacob tried to work a deal with God ("Bring me safely home and I'll give you ten per cent of what I make."), but had to learn to listen more carefully to what God was actually promising him (Genesis 28:20–22 and the rest of the Jacob stories).

Moses had many conversations with God, complaining (Exodus 5:22–23); asking for help (Numbers 28:15–22); arguing – often successfully (Numbers 14:11–20).

The boy Samuel learnt that a voice that called in the night could be God (1 Samuel 3:1–18).

## *Meeting God Can Be Very Simple – Perhaps!*

Meeting God can be very simple. If it is not simple, and no voice speaks in our silence, and no hand reaches down to meet ours in trust, then we should ask ourselves these questions, for the mistake may be ours.

Perhaps God cannot be Himself to us, because we are

not ourselves, our true selves, to Him. We have not prayed to Him as we are, but as we feel we ought to be, or as others want us to be, or as what we think He thinks we ought to be. This last is the most difficult to unravel because it hides a confusion or a blasphemy.

Perhaps God meets us and we do not recognize Him. He may speak to us in a chance remark we overhear, through a stray thought in our mind, or by a word from the prayerbook that resonates in us. Perhaps a side door is the only door we have left open to Him. The others we defended and barred, so He must steal into us as a thief in the night.

Perhaps we do not like what He says, but are frightened to say so, and so pretend we never met Him, and indeed could not meet Him for He is only an idea. The avoidance is natural because in the sight of God our success can seem failure, and our ambitions dust.

Perhaps we are satisfied with our lives and do not want to meet Him. So we chant our prayers and sing our hymns to prevent a few moments' silence, for He speaks in the silence.

Perhaps we have not allowed God to judge us because we have already judged Him, and anticipated His word. He may love us more than we know; He may know us better than we know ourselves; He may still surprise us.

Perhaps we are frightened where He may lead us. He may send us from our father's house; He may bring us to the wilderness; He may let us wander in it for forty years; He may ask us to find our security in what we cannot touch. Will he give us courage equal to our need if we pray?

Meeting God can be simple, but nothing can happen if

we do not will it. If we seek the Lord He can be found; He will allow us to find Him if we seek Him with all our might.

## *Defining Our Relationship With God*

In the love letters of Eloise and Abelard, Eloise tries to define their relationship. You are this but not that, she distinguishes time after time. Well, the Jews tried to do the same with God and came up with this hymn:

For we are Your people and You are our God.
We are Your children and You are our father.
We are Your servants and You are our master.
We are Your community and You are our portion.
We are Your inheritance and You are our destiny.
We are Your flock and You are our shepherd.
We are Your vineyard and You are our keeper.
We are Your work and You are our creator.
We are Your beloved and You are our friend.
We are Your own and You are our nearest.
We are Your people and You are our king.
We are the people known to You and You are the God made known to us.

Why not define how you and God stand in relationship to each other?

I am Your . . . and You are my . . .

Off you go! When you work it out, the complexity of the relationship might surprise you if you're honest about it.

## *When You're Angry With God*

It is sometimes suggested that the God of the Old Testament is an angry God, always chastising and punishing people. That's only part of the story, for the Hebrew Bible is also full of God's love. Nevertheless a lot of emotions do fly around and as often as not, people are angry with God as much as the other way round.

Abraham couldn't understand how a God of justice could possibly punish innocent people along with the guilty in the city of Sodom, and made no bones about it:

> Will you sweep away the righteous with the wicked? . . . That's hardly what You should be doing – shall not the Judge of all the earth do justly?
>
> Genesis 18:25

Jonah was also pretty annoyed about being sent to call his enemy, the Ninevites, to repent – knowing that God was quite likely to forgive them. In exasperation he spits God's qualities of mercy back into God's face:

> Isn't that just what I said when I was back home? I knew You were a gracious and merciful God, endlessly patient and loving and forgiving wickedness!
>
> Jonah 4:2

The prophet Jeremiah has a more personal grudge – because God seems to abandon him just when the going gets tough, so he ends up cursing the day he was born. Job, who is tested by God to the limits of human endurance, takes a Psalm and turns it inside out in his anger. Psalm 8 describes the wonder of God's concern for human beings:

> What is man that You remember him,
> the son of man that You visit him?

Job rewrites it:

> What is man that You elevate him,
> setting Your heart upon him,
> remembering him every morning,
> testing him out every moment!

Perhaps the most recognizable experience is that of Naomi, who loses her husband and two sons and goes into a deep depression: "Why call me Naomi ('pleasantness'), call me Mara, ('bitter'), for the Almighty has embittered me." But calling out her anger against God is the first step of her return to normal life.

So if anger is there – let it out in prayer. God can take it. And maybe He prefers an honest rage that can lead to healing, to an insincere submission that merely bottles up our anger. Sooner or later we'll take it out on someone else or ourselves.

## *My Truest Friend – or What You Will*

LB says:

I was born in the Great Depression and this was a difficult time for normal family life. As a result, God as father or mother doesn't turn me on. Too many problems are associated with these roles. In prayer, I think of God as sister or brother (I've never had either) or friend (I've had a lot, and it's the most successful relationship I know).

Occasionally I also think of God as lover, Rabbi, creator, beggar or child – never in macho images like King, Judge or Lord of Hosts – they are my turn-off.

If you hesitate about thinking of God as a woman, well there are quite a few feminine images in tradition.

> As a mother comforts her child,
> so will I comfort you.
>
> Isaiah 66:13

> I have kept silent for too long,
> kept still and restrained Myself.
> Now I will cry out like a woman in labour.
>
> Isaiah 42:14

> Can a woman forget the baby at her breast,
> show no love for the child of her womb?
> Even these may forget,
> but I will not forget you.
>
> Isaiah 49:15

> Never leave me, never desert me,
> God of my safety.
> Even if my father and mother desert me
> God will care for me still.
>
> Psalm 27:9–10

## *No*

There is always a risk that when we pray we are only willing to "hear" the answer that we want. In that case we are listening to ourselves and not to God. That seems to be what happened to Balaam in the Bible (Numbers 22) where God seems to keep changing His mind, but the conflict of interest is really inside Balaam. The following piece from a modern teacher is a timely reminder about wishful thinking.

> God must also be thought capable of saying "No!". Perhaps this is indeed the major difference between engaging in magic and engaging in prayer. Magic, by definition, *must* work. If it does not yield results, then, in the view of the practitioner of magic, something must have gone wrong with the performance of the magical rite; and he will repeat the rite in a more careful and meticulous manner. Prayer, on the other hand, is addressed to a God who has a will and a mind of His own. God cannot be manipulated by man. He can only be *addressed*. He may, or may not, grant a specific request. But there is no mechanism of man's devising which would compel Him to do so. In addressing God, man knows that a "No" can be as much of an "answer" as a "Yes".
>
> Jakob J. Petuchowski

## *Unholy Thoughts*

## *Curses*

Curses are closely related to blessings – they are blessings turned inside out. And if you can do one, you are capable of the other. Balaam was paid to curse but his curse turned into a blessing. You can read the story yourself in Numbers 22–24.

Curses which express the bad feelings also get rid of them. So they can be as effective as hours of kneework and contrition – and much more fun, provided they make you giggle at your own feelings, even if somewhat nervously.

Unfortunately the curses in the Bible do not have that saving grace. In our time people have experienced the horrors described in Leviticus 26 and Deuteronomy 28. Things will be so bad that "in the morning you will say, 'if only it was evening', and in the evening, 'if only it was morning' because of the dread in your heart and the horrors your eyes are seeing." (Deuteronomy 28:67)

However, humour is never far away and Yiddish, the language of the Jews of Eastern Europe, is capable of marvellous curses:

May you turn into a cheesecake and may he become a cat, and may he swallow you up and choke to death on you!

May you own a large business and may you never have what is asked for and may you never be asked for what you have!

May you own a hundred houses and in each a hundred

rooms and in each room a hundred beds and may you never get a moment's sleep in any of them.

May all his teeth fall out except one, and may that have toothache.

## *Excluded Bits*

Everybody can find him- or herself in the Book of Psalms.

Rabbi Nachman of Bratzlav

Unlike most modern prayers, the Psalms express hate, anger, triumph and bitterness, as well as piety, pity and love, which is why modern psalters sometimes offer them in an expurgated version. Since hate, anger and bitterness are part of a human experience, it's worth seeing what effect these rejected bits have on you. Just because we're shocked by what goes on inside us, doesn't mean we've got rid of it. It's part of us. Perhaps it's better to pray it through.

If only You would kill the wicked, God,
so that those who shed blood would leave me,
those who deliberately defy You,
Your enemies who claim to follow You.
Do I not hate those who hate You, God,
and loathe those who rise against You;
I feel a perfect hatred against them,
counting them as my enemies.

Psalm 139:19–22

The following is fun, but not very nice. Please skip it if you wish to!

> May his days be few;
> may another seize his goods!
> May his children be fatherless,
> and his wife a widow!
> May his children wander from their hovels,
> begging in search of bread!
> May his creditor seize all he has;
> may strangers plunder his possessions!
> Let no one show him kindness
> nor pity his fatherless children!
> May his posterity be cut off,
> may his name be blotted out in the next generation . . .
> He loved to curse, let curses come on him!
> He never wished to bless – may blessing be far from him.
>
> Psalm 109:8–13, 17

## *Religious Traps*

Check your prayer life for
- megalomania
- pardon me for living
- I'm nothing – really!
- rehashing what's happening in the world
- inflation, i.e. blessing too many people you don't know or care about
- monomania, i.e. rabbiting on about yourself
- endless repetition
- asking God for advice and then telling Him what it is

– false piety and righteous indignation
– spiritual snobbery
– your own selection . . .

## *Prayers For People Who Don't Know How To Pray*

If we belong to a particular religion we tend to feel we should use its traditional forms of prayer, because they are the only "proper" way to approach God. But sometimes they don't seem to work for us, and sometimes we have been so far away from them that we don't know quite what to do – so we stay away for fear of making fools of ourselves.

Tradition also knows stories about those who did not know the official prayers, but still managed to communicate directly with God.

One Chasidic story tells of a little boy who went to the Synagogue on the Day of Atonement and stood at the back, embarrassed that he could not join in. He stayed there the entire day, unable to take part, until he felt so desperate that he said to God: "The one thing I know how to do well, God, is to whistle. So let me whistle for you." He let out a piercing whistle which horrified all the other worshippers. But the Rabbi hushed them, and said, "the Gates of Prayer were closing, and our words had not been heard – but this boy's whistle broke through to God for us all."

In another version, a man who could not read the prayers felt equally desperate. So finally he said to God: "I can't read the prayers to You, but at least I know the alphabet. So I will recite that, and You will know how to put the letters together and make the prayers You want to hear."

In matters of prayer to God, we are all ultimately illiterate. So use the prayers of your tradition to speak for you, but if you can't don't be ashamed to offer God whatever you can. As the Rabbis said, "One may do much or one may do little. It doesn't matter, as long as you direct your heart to heaven."

## *One-Liners*

Like, "Help!" – the most sincere prayer there is!

It is not necessary to badger God or bore Him with constant repetition. The Rabbis praised Moses for saying the shortest prayer in the Bible, when asking for healing for his sister Miriam: *"el na r'fa na la,"* "Please God heal her". (They also credited him with the longest, forty days and forty nights (Deuteronomy 9:18), but that was on behalf of the entire people of Israel.)

When we approach our heavenly Parent, we often do not become childlike but childish, and we use on God all the tactics insecure children practise on their earthly one – like going back to the beginning if we've made the slightest mistake, or wrong genuflection. It's like not walking on the cracks between paving stones or touching things, and shows not faith in God, but lack of trust, and belief in magic.

Succinct one-liners can often say it all. Here are examples in frequent use:

"Keep my tongue from causing harm!"
"Come into my heart."
"I trust in You."
"Keep me going!"
"My rock and my redeemer!"
"I love You."

## *Odd Prayers*

Sandwiched in the traditional Grace after Meals is this supplication:

> May we never be in need of the charity of flesh and blood, nor of their loans.

A sincere prayer, obviously, probably reflecting a bad experience on the part of the writer, whoever he was. An intriguing sequel to chicken soup, ice-cream etc.

In the middle of the Day of Atonement, the most solemn of days, the High Priest used to enter the Holy of Holies, the most sacred part of the Temple. When he emerged later, he would say a special blessing calling on God to bring blessing to the land and its harvest. At the end he would add a prayer for those who lived in the region of Sharon, in danger of earthquakes.

> Lord our God, and God of our ancestors, do not let their homes become their graves.

That would be a useful prayer today in many places, especially where civilian populations come under bombardment.

Jewish law forbids doing anything to hasten someone's death, even if they are terminally ill. But you are allowed, even expected, to pray to God for their speedy release from suffering – which is important, because such thoughts can often make us feel guilty.

Some of the paradoxes of prayer are summed up in this one by Al-Harizi who lived in Spain in the thirteenth century:

> Forgive me, God, for what cannot harm You, and give me what I cannot take away from You.

# *Amen*

## *We Put Our Hope In You*

This is the prayer which closes services. It is the most universalistic of the traditional prayers, extending the rule of God to all, however God is understood. Even if you are not comfortable with "God language", you may be able to identify with the hopes it expresses for harmony among the peoples of the world.

Therefore, Lord our God, we put our hope in You. Soon let us witness the glory of Your power; when the worship of material things shall pass away from the earth, and prejudice and superstition shall at last be cut off; when the world will be set right by the rule of God, and all mankind shall speak out in Your name, and all the wicked of the earth shall turn to You. Then all who inhabit this world shall meet in understanding, and shall know that to You alone each one shall submit, and pledge himself in every tongue. In Your presence, Lord our God, they shall bow down and be humble, honouring the glory of Your being. All shall accept the duty of building Your kingdom, so that Your reign of goodness shall come soon and last for ever. For Yours alone is the true kingdom, and only the glory of Your rule endures for ever. So it is written in Your Torah:

"The Lord shall rule forever and ever."

So it is prophesied:

"The Lord shall be as a king over all the earth.
On that day the Lord shall be One, and known as One."

## *Glossary*

Akiva Ben Joseph (c.50 – c.135 CE) Most prominent of the early generations of Rabbis. He began to study late in life, introduced systematization of law and developed new methods of interpreting the Bible. He supported the *Bar Kochba rebellion against Rome and died as a martyr.

Amen A Hebrew word meaning "to be firm", "reliable". It is said at the end of a blessing or prayer recited by another to *affirm* our commitment to what was said – "so be it!"

Avot D'Rabbi Natan Usually printed in the *Talmud, it is a short commentary on the *Pirke Avot.

Bachya, Joseph Ibn Pakuda (1050–1120) Moral philosopher living in Moslem Spain. Author of *The Duties of the Heart*.

Bar Kochba (d. 135 CE) Leader of a military uprising against Rome in the first century (132–135 CE). He was considered by some to be the *Messiah but his defeat proved disastrous.

Berachot (Blessings) A chapter in the *Talmud dealing with the recital of daily and Sabbath prayers.

Bomze, Nachum (1906–54) Yiddish poet. Served with the Red Army. Emigrated to the USA.

Buber, Martin (1878–1965) Vienna-born philosopher,

Bible scholar and religious thinker, best known for his popular books on *Chasidism and his philosophy of dialogue, expressed in his work *I and Thou*. Settled in Palestine in 1938, he was a passionate advocate of Jewish-Arab understanding.

Bunam of Psysha, Simcha (1765–1827) *Chasidic Rebbe with intellectual approach who taught inwardness.

Chasid, Chasidic, Chasidim A popular pietist and mystical Jewish movement that developed in Eastern Europe in the eighteenth century.

CE (Common Era) A Jewish term for the current era, equivalent to the Christian AD, Anno Domini. BCE – Before the Common Era, equivalent to BC.

Day of Atonement (Yom Kippur) A day of fasting and prayer, occurring ten days after the Jewish New Year, for "affliction of souls" and "atonement for sins". It concludes the Ten Days of Penitence when a person's deeds of the past year are weighed in the balance and the judgment is recorded and sealed in the Book of Life.

Genesis The first book of the Bible which tells the story of the Creation of the world, the first human beings and the family of Abraham, chosen by God to bring blessing to the world.

Genesis Rabbah A collection of *Midrashim, Rabbinic legends and commentaries on the biblical book of *Genesis.

Hakotun, Rabbi Moshe A legendary *Chasidic figure to whom many sayings are ascribed.

Heschel, Abraham Joshua (1907–72) American Conservative Rabbi, scholar and theologian. Professor of Jewish Ethics and Mysticism at the Jewish Theological Seminary of America, and a great champion of civil rights. Author of *God in Search of Man*, *The Prophets* and many other important religious books.

Hillel A first-century teacher (before the title "rabbi" was used). Born in Babylon, he became a leading authority in Jerusalem on the interpretation of Jewish law. Renowned for his humanity and ethical teachings, for his formulation of the Golden Rule and the leniency of his legal decisions.

Holtz, Barry Contemporary American poet and essayist.

Hosea An eighth-century BCE biblical prophet in the Kingdom of Israel. Prophesied exile because of the people's corruption, whilst also stressing the continuance of God's love.

Isaiah Prophetic book of the Bible, now thought to be at least two separate works. First Isaiah (chapters 1–39) written in eighth-century BCE, Jerusalem and Second Isaiah (chapters 40–66) written in the sixth-century BCE Babylonian exile.

Job Book of the Bible written in the sixth century BCE in which humanity, in the person of Job, wrestles with the problem of the suffering of the innocent.

Judah The Prince, Rabbi (Hanasi) Living in the second half of the second century and the beginning of the third century CE, he was the Patriarch, the leading religious and political authority, of Judea, and editor of the Mishnah, the first great codification of the Jewish law.

Lamentations Biblical book of five chapters of eulogies and mourning over the destruction of Judah, Jerusalem and the Temple.

Levi Yitzchak of Berditchev (c. 1740–1810) *Chasidic leader. His central doctrine was "love for Israel".

Lucas, Alice (1852–1935) British poetess and translator of medieval Jewish religious poetry.

Maimonides, Moses (Rambam) 1153–1204) Philosopher, legal authority and physician. Born in Spain, he settled in Cairo about 1166. One of the greatest legal authorities and philosophers of all time.

Mar Bar Ravina A Babylonian teacher of the fourth century CE, renowned for his saintly character.

Messiah (Anointed) A term originally used of anyone in the biblical period who was anointed on the head with oil as a sign of office – as Priest, King or Prophet. It became used of the descendant of the Royal Family of King David who would one day restore the fortunes of the Jewish people, returning them from exile to their land. Many have been suggested as possible Messiahs over the centuries, but following them has often led to disaster. So Jews are still awaiting his coming; some consider the "Messiah" as shorthand for a redeemed or perfected world. The Chasidim suggested that each of us has a spark of the Messiah in us which we should cultivate.

Midrash Rabbinic interpretation of either legal or homiletical character, sometimes expressed in parables.

Nachman of Bratzlav (1772–1811) *Chasidic Rabbi and

ascetic. Used parables and stories to illustrate his mystical theology.

Niddah (Menstruous Woman) A chapter of the *Talmud dealing with ritual purification for women.

Petuchowski, Jakob Joseph (1925–92) *Reform Rabbi, scholar and theologian. Born Berlin, emigrated to England 1939, settled in the USA 1948. Leading authority on Jewish liturgy and deeply committed to Jewish-Christian dialogue and Jewish-German reconciliation after the war.

Pirke Avot (Sayings of the Fathers) A chapter of the *Talmud, containing a collection of ethical sayings of the Rabbis.

Proverbs Late biblical book, an example of wisdom literature. It includes aphorisms, exhortations to seek wisdom, etc.

Psalms Biblical collection of 150 poems, some anonymous but many attributed to authors. From different periods, some may go back to the time of King David, to whom authorship of the collection is traditionally attributed. Some were probably recited by the congregation, others by individuals. There are thanksgiving psalms, songs of praise, songs in honour of kings, war songs, songs connected with festivals and individual events, etc.

Rabbi Jewish "clergyman". The Rabbi is not a priest but a layman, an authority on Jewish law, as well as being a teacher and spiritual leader.

Reform Judaism A religious movement within Judaism,

beginning in the nineteenth century, that seeks to reconcile traditional Jewish teachings with modern knowledge.

Ruth Late biblical book recounting the tale of how Ruth entered the Jewish people out of loyalty to her mother-in-law Naomi. From her descended King David.

Sabbath The seventh day of the week, Saturday, on which, according to the beginning of the Book of Genesis, God having completed the work of Creation rested. In biblical and later Jewish tradition it became a universal day of rest, for human beings and animals alike, both to celebrate the Creation and to experience the freedom of rest.

Sanhedrin Chapter of the *Talmud dealing with courts of justice and judicial procedures, particularly criminal law and punishments.

Sephardi Jews descending from those who lived in Spain before the expulsion in 1492, as distinct from Ashkenazi Jews who originated in Central or Eastern Europe.

Shammai First-century Jewish teacher (before the term "Rabbi" was used). He founded his own school of legal interpretation, which was known for its strict interpretation of Jewish law in opposition to the more lenient school of *Hillel.

Shema One of the central parts of Jewish prayer affirming the Oneness of God. The opening comes from Deuteronomy 6:4–9, "Hear Israel, the Lord is our God, the Lord is One."

Song of Songs A biblical collection of love songs. From its language it is a late book, though traditionally it is attributed to King Solomon. A highly erotic work, it was celebrated in Jewish tradition as an allegory of the love between God and Israel.

Succah A chapter of the *Talmud dealing with regulations about the Festival of Tabernacles (Succot).

Talmud (Teaching) Compilation of the commentaries of the Rabbis on the Mishnah (the first Jewish legal code) from the second to the fifth centuries of the Common Era, covering both religious and civil matters. A mixture of laws, customs, discussions, stories and obiter dicta, it became the foundation of Jewish practice throughout the world.

Tashlich ("You shall cast") Ceremony held by the sea or by a stream on the Jewish New Year when breadcrumbs are thrown into the water as a symbolic casting away of sins – based on Micah 7:19 "You shall cast your sins into the depths of the sea."

Tuwim, Juljan (1894–1953) Polish poet and satirist. Returned to Poland after the Second World War.

Zalman, Schneor of Liady (The Rav) (1746–1813) *Chasidic master, founder of the system of *Habad* Chasidism – derived from the initial letters of the words *Hochmah, Binah, Da'at* – wisdom, reason, knowledge. He emphasized intellectual rationalism, traditional rabbinic study and mysticism within the Chasidic movement.

## *Acknowledgements*

*What Is Prayer?*
The Martin Buber passage is from *Ten Rungs: Hasidic Sayings* (Schocken Books, New York 1947), p. 27.

*Dressing*
The Malka Heifetz Tussman passage is from *Midstream* magazine (Vol. 25, No. 5, 1979), p. 35.

*Undressing For Bed*
The Nachum Bomze poem is from *The Golden Peacock*, edited by Joseph Leftwich (Robert Anscombe & Co Ltd, London 1939), p. 267.

*Prayers When You Wake Up At Night*
The Juljan Tuwim poem is from *A Treasury of Jewish Poetry*, edited by Nathan and Marynn Ausubel (Crown Publishers Inc, New York 1957). It is reprinted by permission of Random House Inc, New York.

*For Machinery*
The Barry Holtz poem is from *Response* magazine (Issue 24, Summer 1974), p. 39f.

*Where is God?*
The Martin Buber passage is from *Tales of the Hasidim: The Late Masters* (Schocken Books, New York 1948), p. 277.

*No*
The Jakob J. Petuchowski passage is from *Understanding Jewish Prayer* (Ktav Publishing House Inc, New York 1972), p. 40.